CHAPTER 1

A New King

'Qin is strong,' Li Si *said to the young king.*
'Your enemies are weak. You can be king of every'hin...

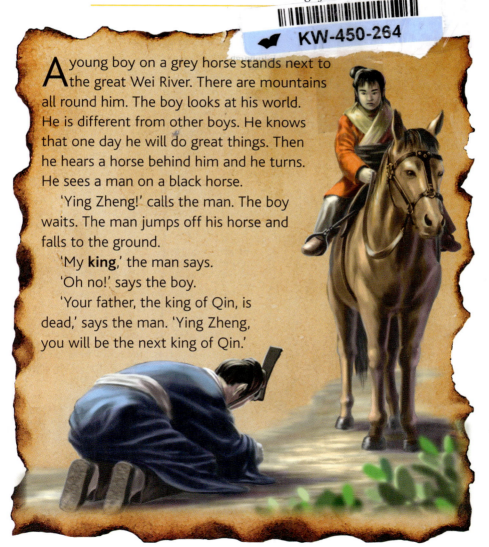

A young boy on a grey horse stands next to the great Wei River. There are mountains all round him. The boy looks at his world. He is different from other boys. He knows that one day he will do great things. Then he hears a horse behind him and he turns. He sees a man on a black horse.

'Ying Zheng!' calls the man. The boy waits. The man jumps off his horse and falls to the ground.

'My **king**,' the man says.

'Oh no!' says the boy.

'Your father, the king of Qin, is dead,' says the man. 'Ying Zheng, you will be the next king of Qin.'

king /kɪŋ/ (n) The *king* is the most important man in his country. His country is his *kingdom*.

The Seven Warring Kingdoms: China in 246 BC*

In 246 BC, there was no China. There were seven kingdoms. From 475 BC to 221 BC, they were all at war. Sometimes two kingdoms fought a third kingdom.

The kingdoms did not only fight. They bought and sold things. They had new ideas about farming. They learned more about their animals. They made new **weapons**. Their scholars talked about **laws** and good **government**. But war was very important to these countries.

'Only fight when you can win,' said one book on war. 'Plan well. Hit your enemy

CHINA

Key

■ Ying Zheng **became** the boy-king of **Qin** /tʃɪn/ in 246 BC. Qin was the strongest of the seven kingdoms.

■ **Yan** /jæn/ and ■ **Zhao** /dʒaʊ/ built great walls round their kingdoms.

■ There were wide rivers and high mountains round **Qi** /tʃiː/. These made Qi strong.

■ **Wei** /weɪ/ and ■ **Han** /hæn/ were in the middle of the warring kingdoms, with other kingdoms to the north, south, east and west.

■ **Chu** /tʃuː/ had a strong and clever prime minister. His name was Chunshen. But when a **palace enemy** killed Chunshen in 238 BC, Chu became weak.

---

* BC: years before Christ was born

weapon /ˈwepən/ (n) You fight with a *weapon*. A gun is a weapon.
law /lɔː/ (n) A *law* says that something is right or wrong.
government /ˈgʌvəmənt, ˈgʌvənmənt/ (n) The *government* makes the laws for a country. It *governs* the country.
become /bɪˈkʌm/ (v) When you change from a girl into a woman, you *become* a woman.
warring /ˈwɔːrɪŋ/ (adj) When one country fights another country, they are *warring* countries. The two countries are fighting a *war*; they are *at war*.
palace /ˈpæləs/ (n) A king lives in a *palace*.
enemy /ˈenəmi/ (n) Your *enemy* wants to hurt you.

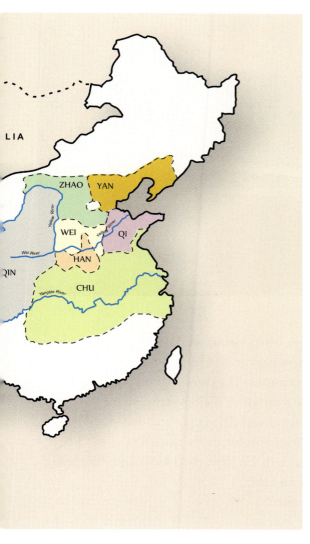

quickly, when he is not ready.'

The kingdom of Qin was in the west. It was in a good place. It had rivers and mountains to the east and a wall to the west. The other kingdoms did not like Qin.

'The people of Qin are not intelligent and they are only interested in money,' people in the other kingdoms said.

They were wrong. The people of Qin were very intelligent.

Of all the kingdoms, Qin was the strongest. The government worked well. It **controlled** the people. The Qin farmers worked very hard too. There was food for everybody and families had many children. The children went into the army.

The Qin **army** moved cleverly and quickly. The soldiers walked 50 kilometres a day with heavy weapons and three days' food on their backs. They were very strong. Qin wanted to be the best.

And when Ying Zheng and Li Si wanted to take the other kingdoms, Qin was ready.

control /kənˈtrəʊl/ (v) When you speak, people have to listen. In this way, you *control* them.
army /ˈɑːmi/ (n) There are many soldiers in an *army*; they fight for their king or country.

● The boy-king

Ying Zheng was only thirteen when his father died in 246 BC. A boy of thirteen could not govern the kingdom of Qin. Zheng turned to his mother, Zhaoji, and his prime minister. The prime minister's name was Lu Buwei and he was as kind as a father to the boy-king. Some writers say that he was his father. Lu Buwei and Zhaoji governed for the boy-king. Lu Buwei won wars and made problems for the enemies of Qin. He invited scholars to the Qin court. He took their ideas and put them in a book. 'These are my ideas,' he said.

The boy-king studied and waited.

● The man from Chu

One day, a stranger arrived at the Qin court. His name was Li Si and he was a student of government from the kingdom of Chu. He liked Qin. 'It wants things and it gets them,' he said to his teacher in Chu. 'The king of Qin wants to be king of the world … that is the place for me.'

So he went over the mountains to Qin. Lu Buwei liked Li Si. Lu Buwei was busy with the kingdom and he wanted a new teacher for the boy-king. Li Si was clever and he was excited about the job. Lu Buwei gave it to him.

● 'Watch and wait'

Ying Zheng was twenty. At twenty, a boy became a man and took a wife. Ying Zheng could become king. 'Now I will lose control,' thought Lu Buwei. 'I have to think of a plan.'

Ying Zheng's grandmother died suddenly. She was very young. Did somebody kill her? Did Lu Buwei kill her?

'Ah, now you can't be king,' Lu Buwei told Ying Zheng. 'You have to wait six months. The time is not right.' And Lu Buwei looked for a new boy-king. Ying Zheng's mother had two more sons with her lover, Lao Ai. They were younger.

'One of them can be the boy-king,' thought Lu Buwei, 'and then I will be their prime minister.'

But Ying Zheng had friends at court too.

'I am teacher to the boy-king,' thought Li Si. 'Now I want to be the king's prime minister.' Li Si did not want to throw away seven years of hard and careful work. He and Ying Zheng planned for the future.

'Watch and wait,' Li Si said to the boy-king. 'Our time will come. Qin is strong. Qin's enemies are weak. You can be king of everything.'

Huang's story (240 BC)

'Life is hard here in Qin. Things are difficult on my farm. Last year the weather was very bad and I lost everything. I had no food for my family, no food for the animals. I gave everything to the government. Everybody in the village became ill. This year the weather is bad again. "We have to have food for the army," the government says. "Give us more bread. Give us more horsemeat." But that's not easy with the weather …'

2.1 Were you right?

1 Who were these people? Find the right names.

a	the boy-king	Li Si
b	the prime minister	Lao Ai
c	the boy-king's mother	Ying Zheng
d	the lover of the boy-king's mother	Zhaoji
e	the boy-king's teacher	Lu Buwei

2 Think again about your answer to Activity 1.2 on page iv. Which of the people in question 1 above governed Qin for the boy king?

2.2 What more did you learn?

1 Are these sentences right (✓) or wrong (✗)?

a Ying Zheng became the boy-king after his father died.

b The seven kingdoms were only interested in war.

c The kingdom of Qin had the best army.

d Li Si was born in Qin.

e When Ying Zheng became a man, Lu Buwei was a good friend to him.

f Life in Qin was easy for farmers.

2 Talk about the pictures. Why were the seven kingdoms interested in these?

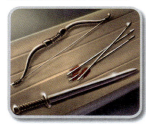
a weapons

b ideas

c farming

2.3 **Language in use**

Read the sentences in the box.
Then finish the sentences below.
Choose a word from each box.

Lu Buwei was **busy with** the kingdom.

Li Si was **excited about** the job.

| afraid | angry | interested |
| different | happy | kind | strange |

| about | about | from |
| of | to | in | with |

1 Ying Zheng is .... other boys. One day he will be king.

2 The kingdom of Qin was not .... the other warring kingdoms.

3 The people of Qin were not only .... money.

4 Lu Buwei was .... Zheng when he was young.

5 Lu Buwei was .... the new teacher from Chu.

6 Zheng's grandmother died suddenly. There was something .... that.

7 Huang was .... the weather and the government.

2.4 **What happens next?**

1 Lu Buwei wants to control Qin. Li Si also wants to control Qin. Who will win, do you think? How?

2 Look at the picture of Zhaoji and her lover, Lao Ai, on page 8. They are making a plan. Which of these people do they want to kill, do you think? Why?

| Lu Buwei | Li Si | the boy-king |

CHAPTER 2

Always at War

'I am not interested in the old ways,' the king of Qin told the world.
'And nobody can stop me!'

Ying Zheng is 21, and now he is king. Qin has many enemies outside the kingdom. Ying Zheng has enemies inside his family.

Lao Ai, the lover of Ying's mother, has big plans. Zhaoji and Lao are in their palace, with their two young sons. Ying Zheng does not know about these half-brothers.

'I am going to kill Ying Zheng,' says Lao. 'Now he is king, you are not important, Zhaoji. When he learns about our sons, he will kill them. I have 4,000 men. I will take them to Zheng's palace, and we will kill him.'

'And the prime minister?' says Zhaoji.

'Lu Buwei? We won't tell him,' answers Lao. 'When I am prime minister of Qin, he will die too.'

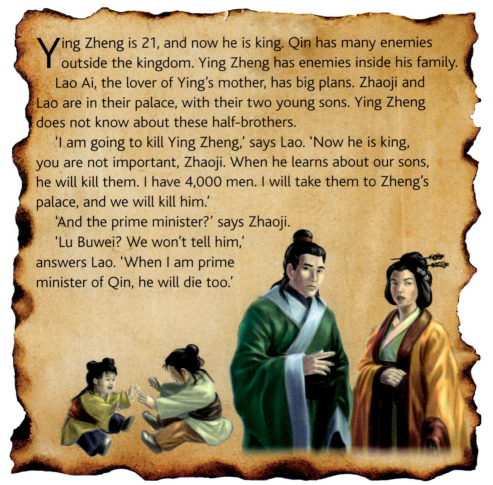

● The end of Lu Buwei

Lao Ai and his small army did not get into Ying Zheng's palace. They fought the king's men in the streets. Many of Lao Ai's men died, and the king sent the other men to the south of the kingdom. They had a very hard life there. The king's soldiers caught Lao Ai. They asked him questions and then killed him and his family. Only Zhaoji did not die, because she was the king's mother.

'How did you meet Lao Ai?' Ying Zheng asked her.

'Lu Buwei brought him to me,' she said.

Ying Zheng was angry with Lu Buwei. He sent his prime minister away from the palace, to a place in the south. He sent angry letters to him there. It was the end for Lu Buwei. In 235 BC, he drank **poison** and died.

Li Si was ready. He took Lu Buwei's place and became the king's new prime minister.

All this taught Ying Zheng an important lesson: 'Everybody is your enemy.'

● The army comes first

Ying Zheng was now a strong king with very big ideas, and his army was very strong too. His soldiers had the same weapons as soldiers in the other warring kingdoms, but they had more weapons, more soldiers and more horses.

Ying Zheng's top army men were very clever. They planned carefully. Before a fight, they sent out soldiers on horses. They watched the enemy carefully. They lit fires under enemy bridges.

Farming was very important in Qin because the army had to have food. Farmers had to give **rice**, fish, vegetables and meat to the army.

● 'Take no prisoners!'

The Qin army moved into Zhao in 236 BC. Zhao was weak and its army could not stop the Qin army. The Qin took 10,000 prisoners. The warring kingdoms always gave prisoners food and clothes. That was

---

poison /ˈpɔɪzən/ (n/v) After you drink *poison*, you are very ill. Often, people die. You *poison* someone when you want to kill them.
rice /raɪs/ (n) We eat *rice* with Chinese food today.

the old way. But Ying Zheng did not follow the old ways. He did not have time for prisoners. He wanted to take the kingdom of Han next. His men killed every Zhao prisoner.

'I am not interested in the old ways,' the king of Qin told the world. 'And nobody can stop me!'

By 223 BC, King Zheng had control of the kingdoms of Zhao and Han. The Qin army turned to Yan. But the king of Yan was ready.

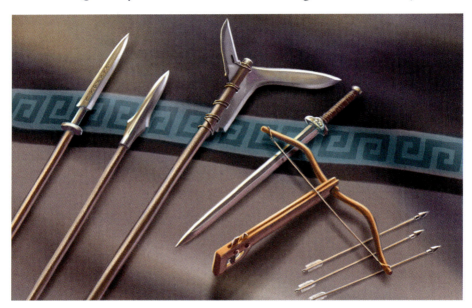

Gao's story (231 BC)

'I come from near the Wei River. I live there with my wife, her mother and father, and our child. We have many horses. We sell them to the army. They use some of our horses for wars and some for food. This year I am sixteen and I have to fight in the army for two years. We are going to fight the Zhao. The Qin army is the best army in the world! We will win! We are the greatest!'

How do we know about China in the time of the First Emperor?

The book: One hundred years after the First Emperor died, Sima Qian, a scholar, wrote a book. The *Shiji* tells the story of China.

Qin laws: In 1975, people found questions and answers about Qin laws in the **tomb** of a government officer. These tell us about life in the empire.

Stone writings: The First Emperor visited the great mountains in his empire. On each mountain he left writings on **stone**. These tell us about his life.

The tombs: Qin kings had large tombs, and the First Emperor's tomb complex was the biggest of all. Ying Zheng took animals, people and many other things into the next world with him.

The terracotta army: Some villagers found the head of a **terracotta** soldier in 1974. First they found one head and then they found an army.

tomb /tuːm/ (n) Some people lie in *tombs* when they are dead. A *tomb complex* has one or more tombs, and other buildings too.
stone /stəʊn/ (n) *Stone* is very hard ground. We often build walls with stones.
terracotta /ˌterəˈkɒtə/ (n/adj) *Terracotta* is red and very hard. You can make plates, cups and other things from terracotta.

3.1 # Were you right?

1 Think back to your answers to Activity 2.4. Who controls Qin now?

2 A Qin minister tells this story to a visitor from Chu.
   Put the words in the box into his story.

> friend   king   caught   streets   prime minister
>   dead   palace   army

'We have a new prime minister. Last month a small ª ....

suddenly came to the king's palace. They were Lao Ai's soldiers – Lao Ai

wanted to kill the ᵇ............................... . His soldiers couldn't get inside

the ᶜ........................... . The king's soldiers ran into the ᵈ...........................

and the two armies fought. Our men won. They ᵉ............................... Lao

Ai and killed him. Lu Buwei was a ᶠ...............................of Lao Ai and now

he's ᵍ............................... too. Li Si is our new ʰ............................... .'

3.2 # What more did you learn?

1 Who dies in Chapter 2? Tick (✓) the boxes.

   Ying Zheng ◯   Zhaoji ◯   Lao Ai ◯   Li Si ◯   Lu Buwei ◯

2 Choose the best words in *italics*.

   a Ying Zheng has a *bigger* / *smaller* army than the other kingdoms.

   b His army has *clever* / *strange* ideas about fighting.

   c The Qin army *never* / *always* gives good food to its soldiers.

   d The seven kingdoms are *usually* / *sometimes* kind to their prisoners.

   e Ying Zheng *is* / *isn't* interested in new ways.

   f Gao *loves* / *hates* fighting with the Qin army.

3 Talk about your country in 221 BC. Who governed it? Was it strong
   or weak? How do people know about life at that time?

3.3 Language in use

**Read the sentences in the box.
Then finish the sentences below
in the same way.**

> 'The Qin army is **the best** army in the world!'
>
> 'We are **the greatest**!'

1 Gao was _the youngest_ soldier in the Qin army. (young)

2 He was in the army for two years and it was .... time of his life. (exciting)

3 Ying Zheng's army was .... in the world. (strong)

4 Horses were .... animals in the First Empire. (important)

5 The *Shiji* is .... book about the Qin Empire. (interesting)

6 The First Emperor left stone writings on top of .... mountains in his kingdom. (tall)

7 The First Emperor's tomb complex was .... of all. (big)

3.4 What happens next?

1 **Life is dangerous for the First Emperor. Why, do you think?
Talk about it and write some ideas.**

2 **Which of these will happen to the emperor, do you think?**

a poison in his food   b a man with a knife   c a stone on his head

CHAPTER 3

The First Emperor

*Jing Ke pulls out the knife. He takes Zheng's arm
and tries to push the knife into him.*

'Qin gets bigger and stronger every year,' says the king of
Yan. 'They want to control Yan too. I'm not going to wait
for their armies. I'm going to hit Qin right at the centre.'

The king of Yan finds a killer. His name is Jing Ke. The king
gives him a small knife inside a map of Yan. There is poison on
the end of the knife. He tells Jing Ke his plan.

Fan Yuchi, an enemy of the king of Qin, lives in Yan. King
Zheng killed his family, and now he wants Fan Yuchi's head.
Jing Ke visits Fan Yuchi.

'Fan Yuchi,' says Jing Ke. 'I will kill King Zheng for you. But
you will have to give your life.'

Life means nothing to Fan Yuchi. He says yes to the plan.
He drinks poison and dies. Jing Ke cuts off Fan Yuchi's head and
puts it in a box.

Then he leaves for Qin.

Jing Ke arrives at the Qin king's palace.

'The king of Yan does not want to fight Qin,' he tells the king.
'I am bringing you the head of Fan Yuchi and a map of Yan.'

King Zheng takes the head and thanks Jing Ke. Then he puts
his hand out for the map.

Jing Ke pulls out the knife. He takes Zheng's arm and tries to
push the knife into him. Zheng jumps back. The king's doctor
throws his bag at Jing Ke. The courtiers call for the king's soldiers.

Five years later, Qin's armies move into Yan.

● China is born

In the six years after Zheng took Yan, many men died. Zheng's armies won control of Wei, Chu and Qi.

In 221 BC, Qin became China and King Zheng, now 38, took a new name. He became Qin Shi Huangdi, First Emperor of Qin.

'I am the first of 10,000 emperors,' said Zheng.

'Long Live the Emperor!' shouted his courtiers.

● Govern from the centre

Li Si and the First Emperor governed in a new way. This way did not change for 2,000 years. Now people had to work hard for a better job. They had to be clever. They did not get a job because they came from an important family.

The Qin city of Xianyang was the centre of the empire, but there were rich families in many other cities in the empire. These families were important in the old kingdoms.

'These families are my enemies. They will start to build armies,' thought Zheng. He brought 120,000 of the families to Xianyang. He wanted to watch them.

Zheng controlled the empire with thirty-six governors. The emperor often wrote to his governors. They could send their ideas to him. So when something happened 250 kilometres away, he knew about it.

Everybody in the empire started to use Qin money. Everybody started to speak the same language and to use the same writing.

A dangerous life

Three times, people nearly killed the emperor. Each time, they got very near to him.

Jing Ke was the first. Then, in 220 BC, a famous musician came to the palace. He played for Zheng. But the musician was a friend of Jing Ke. Suddenly he stopped playing. He jumped up and hit the emperor hard. The emperor's men caught the musician and took him away.

And in 216 BC, the emperor went out for a walk in Xianyang. He wore a workman's clothes. Four of his soldiers walked behind him. They also wore workmen's clothes. The people in the streets did not know their emperor. Three men walked behind him. Suddenly they jumped on him. They wanted his money.

The emperor's soldiers killed the three men. But after that the emperor saw enemies everywhere.

Five journeys

The emperor wanted to see his empire. He wanted his people to see him. He made five long journeys of many months. He visited the highest mountains in the empire. Mountains were important places in those times, because they were the homes of the **gods**. On some of the mountains Zheng left a large stone. The stones told people about his life.

Xia's story (218 BC)

'I am the tenth wife of the First Emperor. I have a son. His name is Hu Hai. The emperor has twenty sons. My son is the eighteenth.

'We have a wonderful palace. My rooms look over the Wei River and across the empire. There are beautiful pictures of birds, flowers and animals on the walls.

'Everybody wears something black at court. Black is the colour of the Ying family and the colour of the empire. Six is the number of the empire, so there are six of everything. Six girls look after me. I have six black horses.

'But we are never in our beautiful palace! Many enemies want to kill my husband. Now we are always moving round the empire. We never stop. I get very tired.'

god /gɒd/ (n) Many people think that a *god* or gods control our lives.

4.1 Were you right?

1 Look back at Activity 3.4. Which of the three things happened to the emperor?

2 Look at these pictures. Which comes first? Write the numbers 1 to 6 in the boxes.

4.2 What more did you learn?

There weren't any newspapers in 221 BC. Men on horses went from city to city and village to village. They told the people about kings and wars. Which sentences, a–d, follow these sentences?

1 'Ying Zheng is the first of 10,000 emperors!'

2 'The enemies of Qin are going to live in Xianyang.'

3 'Everybody in the empire will speak the same language.'

4 'The emperor is starting a new journey.'

   a 'The emperor wants to watch them carefully!'

   b 'Long live the First Emperor!'

   c 'Be ready for a visit!'

   d 'They will use the same money too.'

4.3 Language in use

Read the sentences in the box. Then write *so* or *because* in each sentence below.

> Mountains were important places, **because** they were the homes of the gods.
>
> Six is the number of the empire, **so** there are six of everything.

1 The king of Yan hated King Zheng, ... he sent a killer to his palace.

2 Fan Yuchi hated King Zheng, ... he killed Fan Yuchi's family.

3 The king jumped back, ... he saw Jing Ke's knife.

4 Zheng became emperor, ... he controlled the seven kingdoms.

5 A musician wanted to kill the king, ... he played music at the palace.

6 The emperor wanted to walk in the streets, ... he wore workmen's clothes.

7 The soldiers killed three men, ... the men jumped on the emperor from behind.

8 The emperor wanted to see his empire, ... he made long journeys.

4.4 What happens next?

Read the sentences in *italics* at the top of page 20 and look at the picture on page 21. Then answer these questions.

1 Who are the people in the picture?

....

2 What is happening?

....

CHAPTER 4

One World

'The scholars have a good life here,' he said. 'But now they say that I am a bad man. They will die for that.'

A hundred scholars are sitting on the floor in the palace at Xianyang. The First Emperor comes in. They talk about government.

'In the past,' says one scholar, 'we gave big houses and farms to our old and important families. That was the old way before the Qin Empire. Now we do not do that, and people are not happy.'

'Is the old way always the best way?' asks Li Si, the prime minister.

'The books of Confucius* tell us that this is the right way,' answers the scholar.

'When we did this in the past, what happened?' shouts the First Emperor. 'They built new kingdoms and they fought the king!'

'These books with stories of the past – these are books from the old kingdoms,' says Li Si. 'We are a new empire with new ways. We will have a great fire and we will put these books on the fire.'

'And when we find a scholar with a book of old stories,' cries the First Emperor, 'we will **punish** him. We will send him to the Great Wall.

He will have to build with stones, not words.'

* Confucius (551–479 BC): a great thinker and writer

punish /ˈpʌnɪʃ/ (v) You *punish* somebody after they do something wrong. Parents give *punishments* when their children do wrong.

Fires of books

The First Emperor's men threw the books of Confucius and of the old kingdoms onto fires. But not all books went on the fire. Scholars could study books about war, farming and the law.

But the scholars were not happy. They wanted to read the writings of Confucius. The emperor was angry.

'The scholars have a good life here,' he said. 'But now they say that I am a bad man. They will die for that.'

And in 212 BC, the First Emperor's soldiers killed 460 scholars.

A law for everything

Li Si and Zheng built their empire on laws. There was a law for everything: 'Only five people can live in a house. And only one young man can live in each family.' 'You can only marry one person.' 'Most prisoners get two plates of rice each day, but women and small men can only have one and a half plates of rice.' There was a punishment for everything: 'We will send you to the south of the empire.' 'We will cut off half of your foot.' 'You will work on the Great Wall for five years.' 'Four horses will pull you into four **pieces**.'

Everybody watches everybody

The First Emperor's men looked for enemies of the empire. They watched and listened. They were everywhere and they saw everything. When they caught an enemy of the empire, they cut them in two. Families had to watch other families. Parents had to watch children.

piece /piːs/ (n) When a plate falls on a hard floor, it breaks into many *pieces*.

21

● Build, build, build!

Everywhere in the new empire, there was building.

'When people are busy, they are not fighting,' said the First Emperor.

In ten years, he built 270 palaces in Xianyang. He built palaces round the empire. He made roads, bridges and waterways across the empire. He built the Qin Great Wall, his tomb complex and the terracotta army.

● Ebang Palace

Near the Wei River, the First Emperor built Ebang Palace. The emperor's Great Room was 690 metres wide and 115 metres long. More than 10,000 people could sit in the Great Room. There was a bridge from the palace south to the mountains. There was a bridge north across the river to Xianyang.

'The world will never see a greater palace,' said Zheng to Li Si.

'The world will never see a greater emperor,' answered Li Si.

● The First Emperor's Great Wall

In the time of the warring kingdoms, the Yan, Zhao and Qi built walls round their kingdoms, so there were many walls in the new empire.

The First Emperor liked the idea of walls, but some of them were in the wrong place. He sent his top soldier, Meng Tian, to the north with 300,000 workers. Many of the workers were prisoners. First, they pulled down the walls between the old kingdoms. But they left the walls across the north of the empire, and they built new walls between them. These became one long wall. It was 5,000 kilometres long. The emperor called it the 'Great Wall'.

Why did he want a wall? To the east of the empire, there was the sea. To the south and west, there were mountains. But to the north and west, there were enemies. Dangerous people tried to come into the empire. They wanted weapons, horses and food. They were the Xiongnu. Soldiers watched from the wall. When they saw the Xiongnu, they lit a fire. Other soldiers saw the fire and they lit more fires.

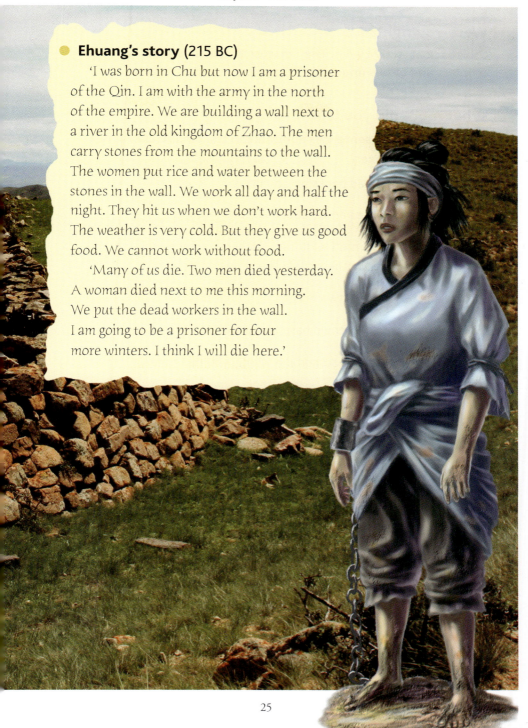

Ehuang's story (215 BC)

'I was born in Chu but now I am a prisoner of the Qin. I am with the army in the north of the empire. We are building a wall next to a river in the old kingdom of Zhao. The men carry stones from the mountains to the wall. The women put rice and water between the stones in the wall. We work all day and half the night. They hit us when we don't work hard. The weather is very cold. But they give us good food. We cannot work without food.

'Many of us die. Two men died yesterday. A woman died next to me this morning. We put the dead workers in the wall. I am going to be a prisoner for four more winters. I think I will die here.'

5.1 Were you right?

Look back at Activity 4.4. Then discuss these questions: Why are scholars and books important? Can we live without them?

5.2 What more did you learn?

1 Which of these sentences about life in the empire are right? Tick (✓) the boxes.

a You couldn't read books by Confucius.

b You couldn't read books about war and farming.

c A family with a mother, father, brother, five children and two grandmothers could live in one house.

d A man could have two wives.

e Women prisoners could have two plates of rice each day.

f When your son did something wrong, you had to tell the emperor's men.

2 Look at this picture. Write laws for this village.

a <u>Do not drive fast in the village</u> ....

b ....

c ....

d ....

5.3 Language in use

Read the sentence in the box and then finish the questions and answers below.

> The emperor's Great Room was 690 **metres wide** and 115 **metres long**.

1 How wide was the emperor's Great Room?

It was ....

2 .... was it? It was 115 metres long.

3 How many palaces did the emperor build in Xianyang?

He built ....

4 .... did he send to the north?
He sent 300,000 workers north with Meng Tian.

5 How long was the Great Wall?

....

6 ....? It was between 3.5 and 7.8 metres high.

5.4 What happens next?

In the time of the First Emperor, people often thought about the next world. The emperor wants to be ready for the next world. What will he do, do you think? Write some ideas.

Notes

CHAPTER 5

The Next World

'Suddenly, one of my brothers shouted and jumped up.
Eyes looked at him from the ground.'

'There is a place in the old stories – its name is Penglai. The old stories say that people there never die. Find Penglai. It is in the sea to the east of China,' says the First Emperor to his court doctor, Xu Fu. 'Bring back **herbs** from there. I do not want to die. I am the emperor. I am Shi Huangdi.'

Xu Fu knows the old stories. 'I have to take 1,000 boys and girls,' he says. 'Then the gods will be happy. They will show me the herbs.'

Xu Fu and his army of young people go to the east of China. They go by boat across the sea and look for Penglai.

The emperor waits for many months. 'Where are they?' he shouts. 'Why aren't they back?' But they never come back.

● 'I do not want to die'

The emperor turned to his other doctors. 'I want to live longer,' he said. 'I do not want to die. What can I do?'

herb /hɜːb/ (n) We use *herbs* in food. We sometimes give people herbs when they are ill.

'We think that the gods drink **mercury**,' they said. 'Try that.' They made a drink from mercury and herbs and gave it to the emperor. In the next seven years, he took more and more.

But mercury was not the answer. It slowly poisoned him. First, he started to talk all the time. He never stopped. Then he became very angry. He saw enemies everywhere. He started to think and do strange things. He could not stay in one place.

'Do not tell anybody that I am here,' he said when he came to a new place in the empire. 'Or I will kill you and your family.'

The next life

The First Emperor was afraid of the next world.

'Many people died in the wars with Qin. Are they all waiting for me in the next life?' he thought. 'When I die, will I meet them?'

He had an idea. 'I will take soldiers with me. When I am in my tomb, my soldiers will be all round me.'

A world under the ground

'I control *this* world,' said Zheng in 221 BC. 'Now I want to control the next world.' He started to build his tomb complex when he was only the boy-king. But when he became emperor, his plans were bigger.

mercury /'mɜːkjʊri/ (n) *Mercury* is a poison. It is thick and shines in the light.

All Qin kings had large tombs. They took many things with them to the next world: wives, food, weapons, clothes and horses. But Zheng's tomb complex was bigger. It was a tomb for the First Emperor of the world.

Workers came from all over the empire and worked on the tomb for more than ten years. In 212 BC, the emperor wanted to finish it. He sent 700,000 more men and women there.

'Work faster,' he said. But they did not finish in time. He died in 210 BC.

Zheng's tomb complex was a palace under the ground. It was a court, an army, a world. There were gardens, mountains and rivers of mercury.

Yang Peiyan's story (1974)

'In the winter of 1973–4 there was no rain. We could not farm without water. In the spring, my brothers and I started to look for water. We found a good place at the bottom of a mountain.

'We worked all morning. We went down one metre into the ground. Suddenly, the ground was red and hard. We tried to cut through it.

'We worked for a week. We broke through the hard ground. Then it was easier again. We found many pieces of terracotta. Were they pieces of old plates or cups? Suddenly, one of my brothers shouted and jumped up. Eyes looked at him from the ground.

'"Look!" he cried. "A man!"

'It was a head, a terracotta head. We pulled it out. Then there were arms, legs, hands, feet! It was a man. It was as big as me!'

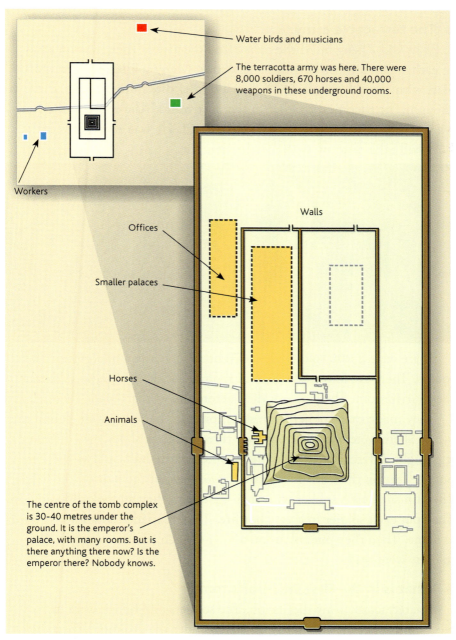

Water birds and musicians

The terracotta army was here. There were 8,000 soldiers, 670 horses and 40,000 weapons in these underground rooms.

Workers

Walls

Offices

Smaller palaces

Horses

Animals

The centre of the tomb complex is 30-40 metres under the ground. It is the emperor's palace, with many rooms. But is there anything there now? Is the emperor there? Nobody knows.

The tomb was in a good place. Mount Li was to the south, the Qinling mountains were to the west, and the River Wei was to the north. The terracotta army looked to the east.

● The terracotta army

Why did Zheng build the palace *and* the army? There was no army in earlier Qin tombs. This was a new idea. Many soldiers died in the wars with the old kingdoms. 'When a soldier dies in this world,' the Qin thought, 'he becomes a soldier in the next world.' The emperor did not want to meet dead soldiers in the next world. He was afraid of them.

'I will take an army with me,' he thought.

There were 8,000 soldiers and 670 horses in three underground rooms. There are four underground rooms, but there were no soldiers in the fourth room. The emperor died before the workers made them.

They made each soldier from seven pieces. The pieces were not all the same. There were two different feet, three different shoes, two different legs, eight different faces. The men worked hard and fast. Two workers put the feet on the legs. The next two workers put the hair on the head. They finished each soldier with their hands, so they all look different. They put each soldier in a very hot fire. The fire made the soldier as hard as stone. Then they put colour on and gave each soldier weapons. The soldiers were ready.

● What is in the First Emperor's tomb?

The terracotta army did its job. The soldiers and horses were in pieces, but nobody went into the palace under the ground. When they open the palace in the future, perhaps we will see the face of the First Emperor of China.

Underground Room 1.
There were 6,000 soldiers in here.

A soldier from Underground Room 2.
There were forty of these soldiers in one place.

There were 8,000 soldiers in the
emperor's army.

6.1 Were you right?

Look back at Activity 5.4. Which of these things did the emperor do?
Tick (✓) the boxes.

1 He ate herbs from Penglai.

2 He drank mercury.

3 He moved from place to place all the time.

4 He built a very big tomb complex.

5 He built a terracotta army.

6.2 What more did you learn?

1 Circle the mistakes in these sentences. Write the right words.

a The workers finished the tomb complex before
the emperor died.   ....

b They worked on the tomb for more than five years.   ....

c The tomb complex was on the top of a mountain.   ....

d The terracotta army soldiers are all the same.   ....

e Today, visitors can see the tomb of the First Emperor. ....

2 How many of each of these were there in the underground rooms?

a ....
soldiers

b ....
horses

c ....
weapons

6.3 Language in use

**Read the sentences in the box.
Then finish the story of the
Yang brothers.**

> He **died** in 210 BC.
>
> We **found** a good place at
> the bottom of a mountain.

1   In the winter of 1973–4 there ...._was_............ no rain. (be)

2   The Yang brothers .... water. (look for)

3   They .... to cut the ground, but it ....
    very hard. (want, be)

4   They .... pieces of terracotta. (find)

5   Suddenly, one of the brothers .... some eyes in
    the ground. (see)

6   They .... a terracotta soldier. (pull out)

7   It .... as big as them! (be)

6.4 What happens next?

Discuss these questions and circle one answer.

1   How will the emperor die, do you think?

   • An enemy will kill him with a knife.

   • He will fall off his horse.

   • He will die in a new war.

   • The mercury will kill him.

   • Li Si will give him poison.

2   Who will take control after the First Emperor dies?

   • His son

   • Li Si

   • Nobody – there will be a war.

   • Enemies from outside the empire

   • The old warring kingdom of Han, Chu or Yan

CHAPTER 6

The Last Journey

He writes to his son, Fu Su.
'You will be the second emperor,' Zheng says. And then he dies.

The emperor is dying. The mercury is killing him. In his sleep he sees a big fish. A sea-god kills the fish. He sees the face of the sea-god. It is *his* face. *He* has to kill the fish.

When Zheng wakes up, he starts on a new journey. He takes his court with him. He goes down the Yangtse River to the sea. He stands on the beach and looks for the big fish. He sees a large fish and kills it. He is the sea-god! He begins the journey back to Xianyang. But he does not arrive there. He becomes ill on the way. The emperor knows that he is going to die. He writes to his son, Fu Su.

'You will be the second emperor,' Zheng says. And then he dies. He is 48.

● The second emperor

The First Emperor wanted his oldest son, Fu Su, to take his place. But Li Si had other ideas. He wanted a younger son, Hu Hai, to be the second emperor. When the First Emperor died, Li Si put the letter to Fu Su on the fire. He took the dead emperor back to Xianyang.

'Hu Hai is the second emperor!' Li Si told the empire.

But only for a short time.

● The last journey

Many people watched the emperor's last journey from Xianyang to his tomb. Soldiers carried him into the centre of the great palace under the ground. The soldiers had to stay with him. The palace builders also had to die because they knew the way into it. The emperor's many wives and horses went inside too.

Then Li Si and his men closed the great doors. They heard the cries of the people and animals. But they did not listen.

● War in the empire

The First Emperor and Li Si did not make many friends when they built their empire. Their government controlled everything and the emperor controlled the government. Everybody in the empire had a job and a place, but many people were unhappy. They did not love their emperor. By the end, nobody liked him. They were afraid of him and his strange ideas. When the emperor died, the government stopped working. The emperor's family, his courtiers, his prime minister and the army all wanted to take control.

● The Han Empire

Eight years of fighting followed. Everybody in Zheng's family died. In 202 BC the Han took control of the empire. The Han scholars wrote the story of the First Emperor. They wanted him to look bad, because he was a Qin. But they used his laws and his ideas of government. They used his language and money. They used his ideas of control. So the empire did not die. It got stronger and stronger.

The terracotta army

There was fighting round Xianyang, at the centre of the Qin empire. The Han soldiers went to the tomb. They found the terracotta army in underground rooms. They took the weapons and broke the soldiers into pieces. Then they started a fire in each underground room. The terracotta soldiers could not fight them. Everybody forgot about the soldiers. Nobody wrote about them. They were there for 2,000 years, in pieces.

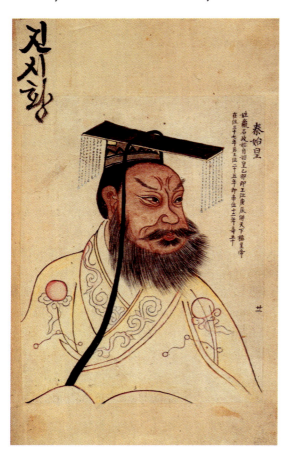

What did the First Emperor leave behind?

When Ying Zheng became king, there were seven kingdoms. When he died, there was one China. People used one language when they wrote. Many other countries learnt from Ying Zheng's ideas for government. We only know half the story of Shi Huangdi. Perhaps when they open the tomb, we will learn the other half.

Important dates

259 BC	Ying Zheng is born.
250	Lu Buwei becomes prime minister to the king.
247	Li Si arrives in Qin.
246	Ying Zheng's father dies and Ying Zheng becomes the boy-king of Qin. He begins to build his tomb at Mount Li.
238	Ying Zheng becomes king of Qin.
238	Lao Ai and his small army try to kill King Zheng.
235	Lu Buwei drinks poison and dies.
234	Qin armies go into Zhao and Han.
230–228	Qin wins control of Han and Zhao.
228	Ying Zheng's mother, Zhaoji, dies.
227	A killer gets into the palace: Jing Ke tries to kill Ying Zheng.
226–221	Qin wins control of Wei, Chu, Yan and Qi.
221	Ying Zheng becomes the First Emperor. He plans a bigger tomb complex at Mount Li.
220	A second killer gets into the palace: The musician hits the emperor.
219	Ying Zheng sends his doctor to Penglai.
213	Li Si makes a fire of books.
212	Ying Zheng kills 460 scholars. He sends 700,000 more workers to his tomb complex.
210	The First Emperor dies.
208	Li Si dies.
206	The second emperor dies. Men break the terracotta army into pieces.
202 BC	The Han Empire begins; Lin Bang is the first Han emperor.
1974	The Yang brothers find a terracotta soldier in the ground.

Talk about it

1 Work with another student. Look at these pictures. These strong men and women also controlled their empires or countries. Learn about them from books or the Internet. How did they die?

Alexander the Great	Catherine the Great	Napoleon	John F. Kennedy
356–323 BC	1729–96	1769–1821	1917–63
1 in bed	**2** a gun	**3** poison	**4** in prison

2 Talk to another student about these pictures. They tell a story from the life of the First Emperor. It happens in 218 BC. What is happening in each picture? Tell the story.

It's a long way to Mount Tai.

A

There's the emperor. Ready ...!

B

Stop him! There he is!

C

Who do you work for? Answer me, or die!

D

The story on page 40 happened in Shandong in the east of the empire. Finish the governor of Shandong's letter to the emperor's ministers. Use these words. Then write your ideas at the end.

kingdoms	soldiers
son	stone	dangerous
head	questions

TO: ALL MINISTERS
FROM: THE GOVERNOR OF SHANDONG
The First Emperor was on the road to Mount Tai in Shandong. We know that this is a ¹................................. road. But the Emperor had many soldiers with him. 'Nobody can hurt him,' we thought. The mountain is high above this road. Cang Hai Gong waited above the road. When the emperor's horses were below him, he pushed a large ²................................. off the mountain. The stone hit the wrong man, thank the gods! The emperor's ³................................. ran up the mountain and caught Cang Hai Gong. They took him to Li Si. Cang shouted at Li Si: 'The Emperor killed many people from the old ⁴................................. Their sons and daughters now want to kill the emperor! He will die!' Li Si asked him many ⁵................................., but Cang pulled away from the soldiers. He ran into a wall and died. The soldiers cut off his ⁶................................. and put it in the middle of the town. Li Si knows now that Cang worked for Ji Ping, the ⁷................................. of the old Han prime minister. Ji Ping ran away before Li Si's men found him. We have to learn more about the emperor's enemies. Why are they unhappy? What can we do about it? Here are my ideas:

• We can ....
  ....
• ....
  ....
• ....

Work with three or four other students. You are going to tell your class about the Great Wall of China.

The First Emperor built the first Great Wall. But the Ming emperors (1368–1644) built a longer and stronger Great Wall. The map below shows the Ming Great Wall. Visitors today see this wall.

1 **Look at this picture of the Great Wall and finish the notes.**

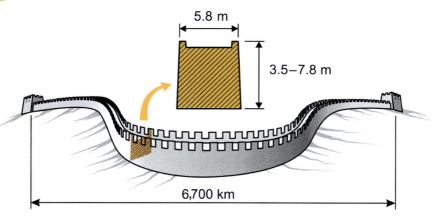

The wall is about ª.. long. In some

places it is ᵇ.......................... wide. It is between ᶜ..........................

and ᵈ.......................... high.

2 Think of questions about the wall and write them below. Then find answers in books or on the Internet. Make notes.

1 How did Chinese emperors use the wall?

....

2 How many people visit the wall each year?

....

3 Can you walk from one end to the other end?

....

4 ....

....

5 ....

....

6 ....

....

3 Read more about the Great Wall. Choose two interesting things for your talk. What are they, in your words?

The Ming 'Radio'

At the time of the Ming empire (1368–1644), soldiers lived on the wall. Their families lived in villages next to the wall. The Mongols lived outside the empire. They wanted to come into the empire and take animals, weapons and food. The soldiers watched for the Mongol armies. When soldiers saw Mongols, they lit a fire. The soldiers in the next village saw the fire. Then they lit a fire too. One fire meant 100 Mongols. Five fires meant 5,000 Mongols. This was the Ming 'radio'. It was faster than a man on a horse.

明朝的無線電通訊

The Great Wall is Falling Down

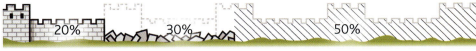

20% 30% 50%

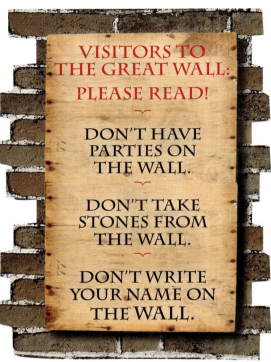

VISITORS TO
THE GREAT WALL:
PLEASE READ!

DON'T HAVE
PARTIES ON
THE WALL.

DON'T TAKE
STONES FROM
THE WALL.

DON'T WRITE
YOUR NAME ON
THE WALL.

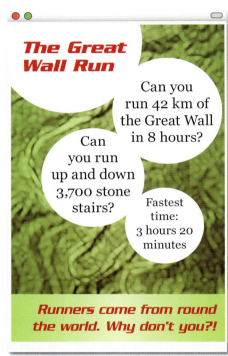

The Great Wall Run

Can you run 42 km of the Great Wall in 8 hours?

Can you run up and down 3,700 stone stairs?

Fastest time: 3 hours 20 minutes

Runners come from round the world. Why don't you?!

4. **Make notes for your talk in your notebook. Then write the talk.**

5. **Give your talk. Ask for questions at the end.**

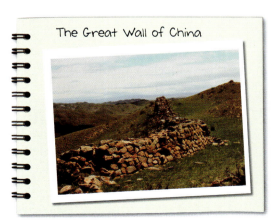

The Great Wall of China